PETER & THE FIRST CHRISTIANS
© 1985 by Multnomah Press
Portland, Oregon 97266

Original edition published in French by Les Editions Sator.,
Pierrefitte, 93380, France.
Copyright © 1985, Les Editions Sator.

Printed in Italy

Library of Congress Cataloging in Publication Data

Lalo, Laurent.
 Peter & the first Christians.

 Translated from the French.
 Summary: Retells the events after Jesus's ascension into heaven which form the basis of the beginnings of the Christian church.
 1. Bible stories, English—N.T. Acts. 2. Bible. N.T. Acts I-III—Comic books, strips, etc.
3. Church history—Primitive and early church, ca. 30-600—Juvenile literature.
4. Peter, the Apostle, Saint—Juvenile literature. [1. Bible stories—N.T.]
I. Title.   II. Title: Peter and the first Christians.

BS551.2.L32   1985   226'.609505   84-42946
ISBN 0-88070-084-X

85 86 87 88 89 90 91 – 10 9 8 7 6 5 4 3 2 1

PETER & THE FIRST CHRISTIANS

ILLUSTRATED BY LAURENT LALO

THE TIME IS THE FIRST CENTURY A.D.
LUKE, A GREEK DOCTOR HAS LEFT HIS WORK
TO TRAVEL AROUND HELPING PAUL,
THE FIRST CHRISTIAN MISSIONARY.

DAY AFTER DAY THEY TEACH PEOPLE
WHO HAVE NEVER HEARD OF JESUS,
ABOUT HIS LIFE, DEATH AND
RESURRECTION.

...FINALLY, LUKE DECIDES TO USE HIS KEEN
DOCTOR'S MIND TO COLLECT TOGETHER ALL
THE INFORMATION ABOUT JESUS, INTO A CLEAR
ACCOUNT. THE BOOK HE WROTE STILL EXISTS.
WE CALL IT LUKE'S GOSPEL.

THE DOCTOR THEN WENT ON TO RECORD
THE EXCITING STORY OF THE EARLY
CHRISTIANS. IT BEGAN WITH ONE MAN
IN PARTICULAR.
HIS NAME WAS PETER.

FIRST UNITED METHODIST CHURCH
311 SOUTH BROADWAY
SANTA MARIA, CALIFORNIA 93454

MULTNOMAH PRESS
PORTLAND, OREGON 97266

AFTER JESUS HAD BEEN PUT TO DEATH BY CRUCIFIXION IN THE CITY OF JERUSALEM, CAPITAL OF PALESTINE, GOD BROUGHT HIM BACK TO LIFE AGAIN. HIS AMAZED FRIENDS WERE ABLE TO WALK, TALK AND EAT WITH HIM FOR A WHOLE MONTH. DURING THAT TIME JESUS TAUGHT THEM ALL HE COULD. THEN HE GAVE THEM A PROMISE — THEY WERE TO WAIT IN JERUSALEM UNTIL THE HOLY SPIRIT CAME TO THEM. THE SPIRIT WOULD GIVE THEM THE COURAGE AND POWER TO PREACH JESUS' GOOD NEWS TO THE WHOLE WORLD.

...FINALLY JESUS TOOK HIS CLOSEST FRIENDS TO A HILL OUTSIDE JERUSALEM AND AS THEY WATCHED IN AWE, HE LEFT THEM, DISAPPEARING INTO THE CLOUDS.

THE DISCIPLES WERE STILL STRAINING TO CATCH A LAST GLIMPSE OF JESUS, WHEN THEY REALISED TWO MEN, DRESSED IN WHITE, HAD JOINED THEM.
"WHY ARE YOU STANDING LOOKING UP AT THE SKY?" THEY SAID, "JUST AS JESUS HAS NOW BEEN TAKEN UP INTO HEAVEN, ONE DAY HE WILL COME BACK AGAIN."

AFTER THESE ASTOUNDING EVENTS,
THE LITTLE GROUP, BEWILDERED AND AFRAID,
RETURNED TO THEIR UNOFFICIAL HEADQUARTERS
-THE ROOM WHERE THEY HAD EATEN A FAREWELL
SUPPER WITH JESUS, BEFORE HIS DEATH.

THERE THEY
WAITED.

THE GROUP HAD GROWN TO ABOUT 120 PEOPLE, INCLUDING JESUS' MOTHER MARY, SOME OTHER WOMEN AND HIS BROTHERS. IT WAS THE JEWISH FEAST OF PENTECOST AND THEY WERE PRAYING TOGETHER.

THIS COSMOPOLITAN CROWD WERE ATTRACTED BY THE COMMOTION IN THE HOUSE. EACH VISITOR WAS AMAZED TO HEAR A GROUP OF ORDINARY JEWISH PEOPLE, SPEAKING ABOUT GOD IN HIS OWN LANGUAGE.

"LISTEN. JESUS OF NAZARETH WAS A MAN SENT BY GOD. HE COULD DO ALL KINDS OF MIRACLES, AS MANY OF YOU KNOW BECAUSE YOU SAW THEM... YET, A FEW WEEKS AGO YOU HAD HIM EXECUTED BY CRUCIFIXION. WELL, GOD HAS BROUGHT HIM BACK TO LIFE. WE HAVE SEEN HIM. NOW HE HAS GONE BACK TO HIS FATHER. WHAT YOU HAVE WITNESSED TODAY IS HIS HOLY SPIRIT. — HIS POWER — COMING UPON US AS HE PROMISED. MAKE NO MISTAKE ABOUT IT, JESUS IS GOD'S MESSIAH!"

ABOUT THREE THOUSAND RESPONDED TO PETER'S WORDS THAT DAY. THE DISCIPLES ACCEPTED THEM GLADLY, BAPTISING THEM IN THE NAME OF JESUS, AS A SIGN THAT THEY HAD BEGUN A COMPLETELY NEW LIFE.

JESUS' FIRST DISCIPLES TAUGHT THE NEW
CHRISTIANS ALL THEY COULD ABOUT HIM.
THEY SHARED A SPECIAL MEAL OF BREAD
AND WINE TO HELP THEM REMEMBER
JESUS' DEATH AND RESURRECTION.

THE GROUP OF CHRISTIANS IN JERUSALEM
GREW FAST. THEY SPENT THEIR TIME MEETING IN
THE TEMPLE AND PRAISING GOD. EVERYONE WAS
IMPRESSED BY THEM.

...AND THEY MET IN EACH OTHER'S HOMES FOR PRAYER AND MEALS TOGETHER.

MANY SOLD THEIR BELONGINGS AND GAVE THE MONEY TO THE GROUP, SO THAT NO-ONE WOULD GO WITHOUT.

GOD WORKED MANY MIRACLES THROUGH THE DISCIPLES AND PEOPLE WERE AMAZED AT THEIR POWER. ONE DAY, AS PETER AND JOHN WERE GOING INTO THE TEMPLE, A CRIPPLED MAN ASKED THEM FOR MONEY.

PETER LOOKED AT HIM. "WE HAVE NO MONEY" HE SAID, "BUT I HAVE SOMETHING TO GIVE YOU... IN THE NAME OF JESUS CHRIST OF NAZARETH, I ORDER YOU TO GET UP AND WALK!"

THEN PETER GRASPED HIM BY THE HAND AND THE MAN STOOD UP!

THE AMAZED MAN TOOK A STEP... THEN TWO... HE COULD **WALK!**

...MORE THAN THAT, HE COULD JUMP AND LEAP.

INTO THE TEMPLE HE RAN, PRAISING GOD AT THE TOP OF HIS VOICE!

EVERYONE IN THE TEMPLE RECOGNIZED THE MAN WHO HAD BEEN DISABLED AND A LARGE CROWD GATHERED ROUND PETER AND JOHN. PETER SPOKE TO THEM.

THAT FIRST GROUP OF CHRISTIANS CONTINUED
TO GROW AND SPREAD THROUGHOUT THE COUNTRY OF
ISRAEL AND BEYOND. BUT THE YOUNG CHURCH HAD ENE-
MIES. PETER ~ LIKE MANY OTHER CHRISTIANS ~ WAS THROWN
INTO PRISON, BUT HE WAS MIRACULOUSLY SET FREE IN
THE MIDDLE OF THE NIGHT.
PETER CONTINUED AS A STRONG LEADER OF GOD'S
PEOPLE FOR MANY YEARS.
THE STORY OF PETER AND THE EARLY CHURCH IS IN
THE BIBLE, IN THE BOOK OF ACTS, CHAPTERS 1 TO 12

© LES EDITIONS, B.P. 580, F-75827, PARIS CEDEX 17, FRANCE
CO-EDITION ARRANGED WITH ANGUS HUDSON, LONDON